CONTENTS

Tyrannosaurus rex had a huge bite.

Its big teeth could crush bones.

Velociraptor could run at least
30 kilometres (24 miles) per hour.

Stegosaurus had bony plates on its back.

Dinosaurs lived millions of years ago.

They were amazing!

Dinosaurs ARE Everywhere!:
COOL FACTS ABOUT THE JURASSIC PERIOD

by Ellis M. Reed

Raintree is an imprint of Capstone Global Library Limited, a company incorporated in England and Wales having its registered office at 264 Banbury Road, Oxford, OX2 7DY – Registered company number: 6695582

www.raintree.co.uk
myorders@raintree.co.uk

Text © Capstone Global Library Limited 2020

The moral rights of the proprietor have been asserted.

Edited by Meg Gaertner
Designed by Becky Daum
Production by Colleen McLaren
Printed and bound in India

ISBN 978 1 4747 7455 0 (hardback)
ISBN 978 1 4747 8240 1 (paperback)

British Library Cataloguing in Publication Data
A full catalogue record for this book is available from the British Library.

Acknowledgements
We would like to thank the following for permission to reproduce photographs: Alamy: Xinhua, 23; iStockphoto: Elenarts, 17, fdevalera, 26–27, HomoCosmicos, 20–21, LeventKonuk, cover (foreground), USO, 18–19, Wlad74, 26; Science Source: De Agostini Picture Library, 12, Francois Gohier, 24–25; Shutterstock Images: Akkharat Jarusilawong, 11, Anurak Pongpatimet, 30–31, Herschel Hoffmeyer, 13, mgfoto, 7, mikluha_maklai, 8–9, Pavel Tvrdy, cover (background), Shvoeva Elena, 5, 15, srulik, 8
Every effort has been made to contact copyright holders of material reproduced in this book. Any omissions will be rectified in subsequent printings if notice is given to the publisher.

We would like to thank Stephanie K. Drumheller-Horton, PhD, Lecturer of Palaeontology, for her help with this book.

Stegosaurus' plates were stuck in its skin, not attached to its skeleton.

Some dinosaurs ate plants. They were **herbivores**. Stegosaurus had a beak and small teeth. It ate bushes and fallen leaves or seeds. Its teeth were not very strong.

Diplodocus was 27 metres (90 feet) long. It had a long neck. It ate leaves from trees.

People can see Diplodocus skeletons in museums.

Some dinosaurs ate meat. They were **carnivores**. T rex ate other dinosaurs. It had tiny arms. But its neck was strong. T rex could toss **prey** in the air.

T rex had 60 teeth, each up to 20 centimetres (8 inches) long.

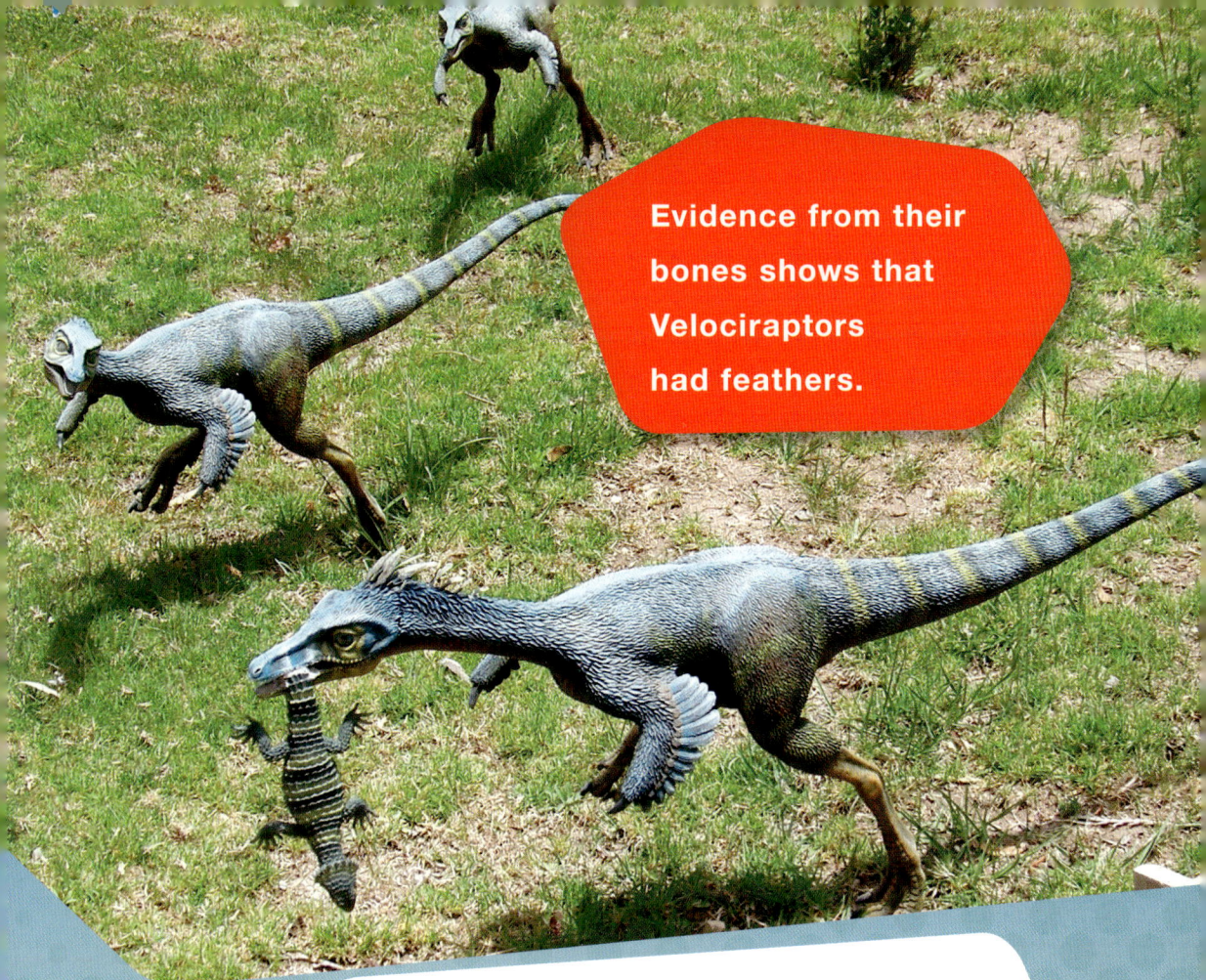

Evidence from their bones shows that Velociraptors had feathers.

Velociraptor ran on two feet. Each foot had a long claw on its second toe. The dinosaur could balance on one foot. Then it slashed with the other foot. This helped it catch food.

Defences

Many dinosaurs had unique features. Triceratops had three horns on its head. It used these horns to fight other Triceratops. The horns might have also helped the dinosaur to attract a **mate**.

Triceratops also had a large frill on the back of its head.

Edmontonias were ankylosaurs. They had large spikes on their necks and shoulders. They used these for **defence**. Other ankylosaurs had clubs on their tails. They used these like weapons.

THERIZINOSAURUS

One dinosaur had the longest claws in history. Its claws were about 1 metre (3.2 feet) long. It used its claws to grab plants. The claws also helped with defence.

Therizinosaurus was a large dinosaur with long arms.

Most dinosaur **species** are **extinct**. They do not exist anymore. But other dinosaurs are still around. Birds are dinosaurs!

Many dinosaurs were like birds.
Some had feathers. Others had hollow
bones. The bones were very light. These
dinosaurs could move quickly.

Coelophysis used its speed to catch small prey.

ARCHAEOPTERYX

Archaeopteryx was a dinosaur. It may also have been the first bird. It lived 150 million years ago. It had three claws on each wing. But it could not fly very well.

A BIRD WITH TEETH

Unlike today's birds, Archaeopteryx had teeth.

Archaeopteryx had wing bones similar to today's quails. Quails can fly in short bursts.

SHARKS

Sharks were around 420 million years ago. Some species did not become extinct. They are still alive today. But the biggest shark lived 2.6 million years ago. Megalodon was a huge shark. It hunted whales and other animals. It grew up to 18 metres (59 feet) long. That is almost three times as big as today's great white shark!

TOOTH CLUES

Sharks' skeletons are made of **cartilage**. Cartilage rarely **fossilizes**. But scientists can study Megalodon's teeth. The teeth tell scientists how big the shark was.

Models of Sarcosuchus show its large mouth.

CROCODILES

Crocodiles lived at the same time as some dinosaurs. One crocodile was called Sarcosuchus. It was 12 metres (40 feet) long. It weighed 8 tonnes. That is heavier than a modern African elephant! Today's saltwater crocodiles are about half this size.

BIG MOUTH

Sarcosuchus hunted on land and in water. It ate small dinosaurs. Its head was almost 1.8 metres (6 feet) long!

FINDING
Fossils

Scientists know about dinosaurs from

fossils. Many of these are old bones.

They can be millions of years old.

Scientists found a fossil in 1994. It was a small dinosaur called Citipati. The fossil was almost a complete skeleton. It was sitting on a nest of eggs.

A model of Citipati shows it near its nest.

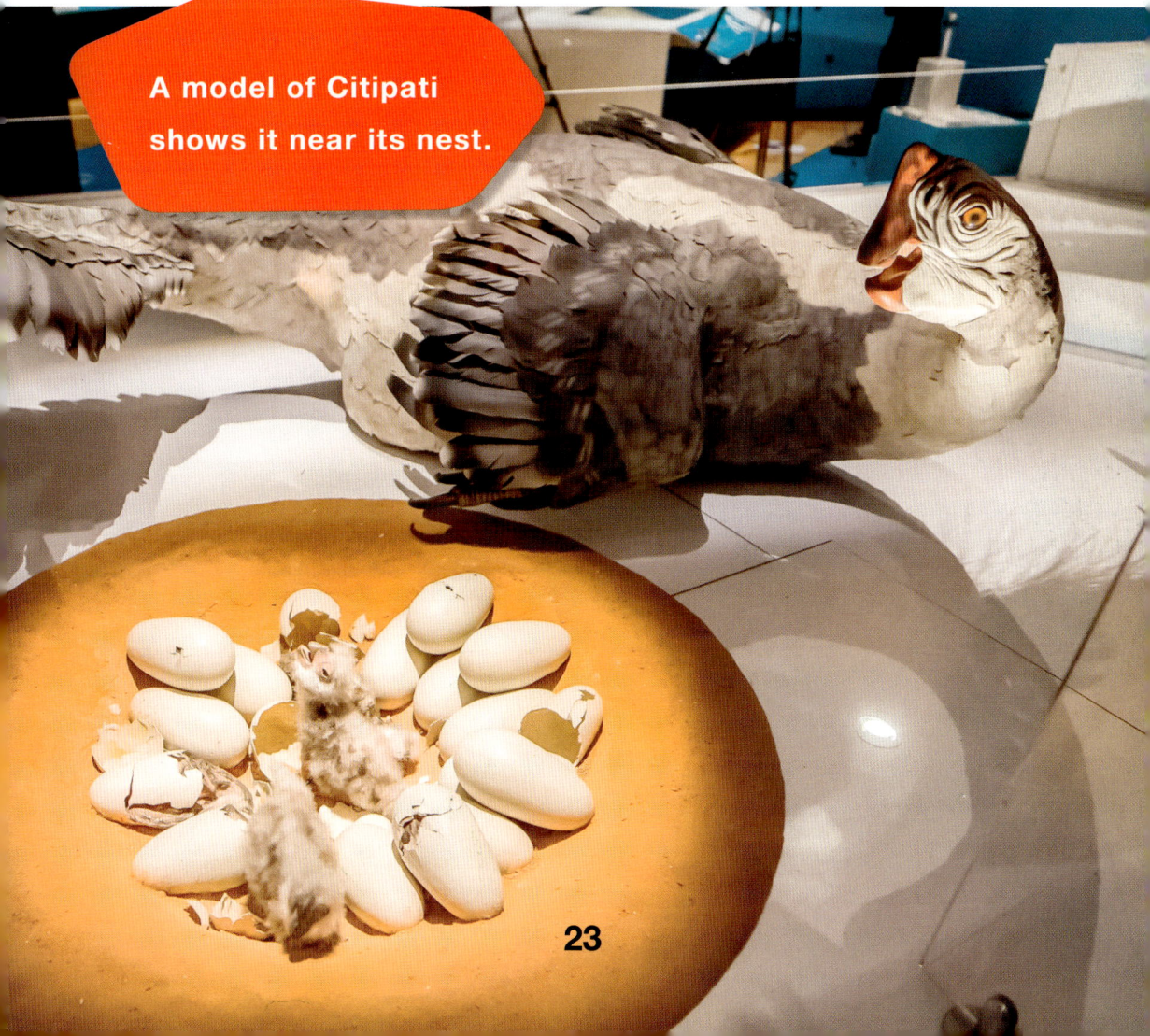

FIGHT TO THE DEATH

Scientists once found a fossil of two dinosaurs fighting. One was a Velociraptor. Its long claw was in the other dinosaur's neck.

The other dinosaur was fighting back. It was a Protoceratops. Its jaws were around the Velociraptor's arm. The two dinosaurs died in this pose.

The fossil is known as the Fighting Dinosaurs.

Archaeopteryx fossils show traces of feathers.

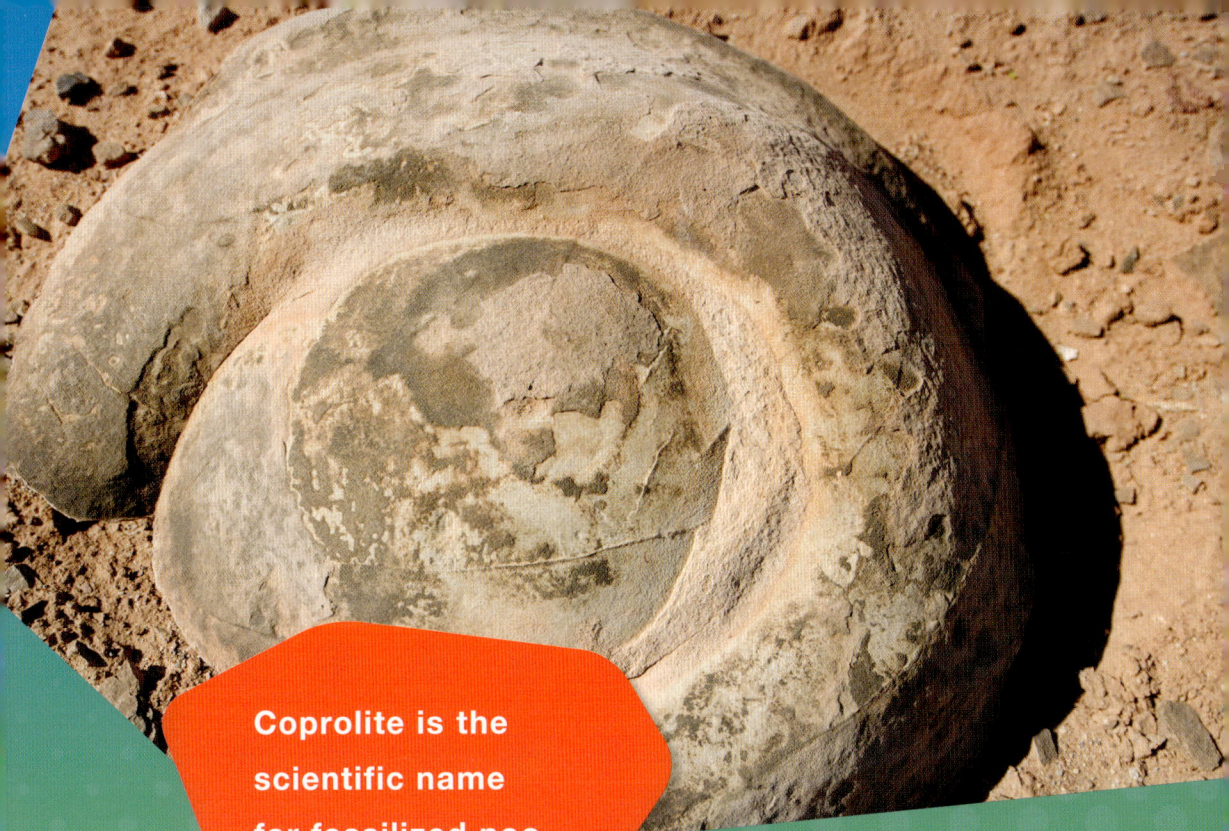

Coprolite is the scientific name for fossilized poo.

Fossils are not always dinosaur bones. There are fossils of dinosaur skin. They show some dinosaurs had scales. Other dinosaurs had feathers. There are even fossils of dinosaur poo!

carnivore
an animal that eats meat

cartilage
flexible tissue that makes u
parts of animal bodies and
softer than bone

defence
self-protection

dinosaur

TRIVIA

1. Scientists do not agree about which dinosaur was the largest. But one of the largest dinosaurs was *Patagotitan mayorum*. It was 37 metres (122 feet) long. It weighed 76 tonnes. That is as heavy as 12 modern African elephants!

2. The smallest dinosaur ever lives today! It is the bee hummingbird. It is only about 5 centimetres (2 inches) long.

3. Some baby dinosaurs were eaten by snakes. The snakes were 3.5 metres (11 feet) long. Scientists found fossils of these snakes next to dinosaur nests.

ACTIVITY

DINOSAUR SCIENTIST

You can be a dinosaur scientist. You can look for fossils or other clues left by animals in your own back garden! Scientists use special tools to dig for fossils. Look online to see what kinds of tools scientists use. These might include soft brushes or picks.

Then, with an adult's permission, see what you can find in your garden. You can brush soil off rocks. Do they have animal footprints or tracks? You can dig into the ground. Are there bones or eggs? Look at what you find. Can you guess what kind of animal left these clues?

FIND OUT MORE

Love dinosaurs? Check out these resources.

Books

Knowledge Encyclopedia: Dinosaur! (DK, 2014)

Dictionary of Dinosaurs, Dr. Matthew G. Baron (Wide Eyed Editions, 2018)

Totally Amazing Facts about Dinosaurs (Mind Benders), Mathew J. Wedel (Raintree, 2019)

Websites

Dinosaurs for Kids
www.kids-dinosaurs.com/dinosaurs-for-kids.html

Natural History Museum
www.nhm.ac.uk/discover.html

DK Find Out!: Dinosaurs
www.dkfindout.com/uk/dinosaurs-and-prehistoric-life/dinosaurs

INDEX